WASHINGTON, D.C.

WASHINGTON, D.C.

THE NATION'S CAPITAL

BY
SAM AND BERYL EPSTEIN

A First Book/Revised Edition
Franklin Watts
New York/London/Toronto/Sydney/1981

Cover Photograph courtesy of:
S.L. Waterman/Photo Researchers, Inc.

Photographs courtesy of:
Washington Convention and Visitors Association:
frontis, pp. 9, 48, 49, 57, 69, 71, 79, 82;
United Press International:
pp. 4, 18, 60, 61;
Culver Pictures:
pp. 12, 28, 45;
Wide World Photos:
p. 25;
National Park Service:
pp. 22, 33, 37, 73, 76;
Library of Congress:
p. 30;
Franklin D. Roosevelt Library:
p. 40;
Paul Conklin/Monkmeyer Press Photo Service:
pp. 53, 65.

Library of Congress Cataloging in Publication Data

Epstein, Samuel, 1909–
Washington, D.C.

(A First book)
Edition for 1961 published under title:
The first book of Washington, D.C.
Includes index.
SUMMARY: An introduction to Washington, D.C.,
its history, day-to-day life, and points of interest.
1. Washington, D.C.—Juvenile literature.
[1. Washington, D.C.]
I. Epstein, Beryl Williams, 1910–
II. Title.
F194.3.E67   1981   975.3   80–25022
ISBN 0–531–04253–7

CONTENTS

WASHINGTON, D.C.

THEY COME TO WASHINGTON

When Washington residents talk about their "home town," they usually mean a town or city in one of the fifty states. Most of them were born and have lived elsewhere before they chose to come to Washington. They complain about its traffic jams, its hot and humid summers, its winters that are damp and cold. But they stay on in the nation's capital because things happen here that could happen nowhere else.

Here the President's helicopter, rising from the White House lawn, is a common sight.

Here members of Congress, often weary and hoarse after long sessions of debate, vote on bills that affect the lives of Americans, and often of people in other lands as well.

Here reporters from all over the world gather to hear a black-robed justice of the Supreme Court read a decision that gives new meaning to one of the most important documents in the history of humanity—the Constitution of the United States.

Here a housewife shopping for her family's dinner discusses meat prices with a visiting home economist from Pittsburgh or Peoria, from France or Formosa.

Here a Boy Scout or a Girl Scout goes camping with the children of foreign ambassadors and the grandchildren of members of the President's cabinet.

These things happen in Washington every day, because Washington is the seat of the government of the United States. That government is the magnet that attracts people to this city and holds them here.

WASHINGTON'S FIRST RESIDENTS

One of the capital's earliest residents was Abigail Adams, wife of John Adams, the second President of the United States. She arrived in Washington on a cold November day in the year 1800 to set up housekeeping in the President's house.

Still unfinished, the big stone building overlooking the Potomac stood among trees and raw stumps. A hole in the ceiling of the wide central hall showed where a staircase would someday lead to the upper floor. Sawdust and piles of lumber littered the corners of dank, chill rooms. The plaster on the walls was not yet dry. The large reception room at the east end of the hall would not be ready for guests for many more weeks. In the meantime, Mrs. Adams thought, while the yard remained a sea of mud she would be able to hang her laundry in the big, bare room.

In that year of 1800, the nation's congressmen and the members of the Supreme Court began working in a small, crowded building they called the Capitol. (The word for a building is always spelled with an *o* in the last syllable, not with an *a* as in *capital*, the word used for the chief city of a state or nation.) The building was actually only one boxlike wing of the Capitol that the federal government planned to build someday.

The 126 clerks and other government employees who made up the entire staff of the government, lived uncomfortably in whatever quarters they could find. The thirty-two senators and 106 representatives were housed no better. They slept in taverns, or cramped boardinghouses in nearby Alexandria or Georgetown. If a senator or a representative wanted to call on the President, he had to slog to the President's house through a mile (1.6 km) or more of muddy woods.

WASHINGTON TODAY

Since the day Abigail Adams moved into the unfinished President's house, thousands of homes and apartment buildings have gone up in Washington. They provide living space for about 700,000 people, of whom about 525,000 are black. Washington has a larger percentage of black residents—over 70 percent—than any other city in the United States. Another 1.8 million people, both black and white, live in Washington's suburbs in Maryland or Virginia.

Every morning many thousands of those suburban dwellers come into the city, by car or bus or Washington's handsome subway, to join the city dwellers for the day's work. Together they staff stores, banks, gas stations, hotels and restaurants, and all the other kinds of businesses found in any large metropolitan area. They operate hospitals, public transportation, police, fire, and sanitation departments. They teach in public schools and many fine colleges.

But about one out of every four workers who live in or around Washington is employed by some branch of the business that has always been the city's biggest—the business of the federal government.

Those 126 employees of the year 1800 would be lost among today's more than 400,000 clerks, lawyers, doctors, scientists, and specialists of all kinds. Federal employees now do more than 1,700 different kinds of jobs. Some 25,000 of them work in one building alone—the 27-acre (10.9-hectare) Pentagon with its hundreds of rooms and 17½ miles (28 km) of corridors.

The second biggest business in Washington today is the business of looking after its visitors. Twenty million or more of them pour into the city every year.

[3]

A station on the new Metro subway
that serves D.C., Virginia, and Maryland.

Families come here for their vacations from every state in the Union and from the farthest corners of the earth.

Groups of students arrive by plane or train, or in special sight-seeing buses that take them on tours of the city.

Members of unions and other organizations come here because their national or international headquarters are in Washington.

Scientists and specialists of all kinds come here to share ideas and information at meetings often called by the government.

All of these people want to see a city that is now famous for its beauty and its many treasures—valuable works of art and priceless documents, architectural wonders and wonders of nature.

But above all most of them want to watch the government of the United States at work.

Sometimes they complain that there is too much to see in this capital that was a wilderness less than two centuries ago. They are afraid they will not have time to see it all. Perhaps that is why they usually want to visit first the two buildings where the elected representatives and leaders of the United States have been working, year in and year out, since the government of the United States moved to Washington in 1800. Those two buildings are the Capitol and the President's house, now officially known as the White House.

FOUR DOORS TO THE WHITE HOUSE

The White House has four entrances.

The big doorway on the north side, under the portico with

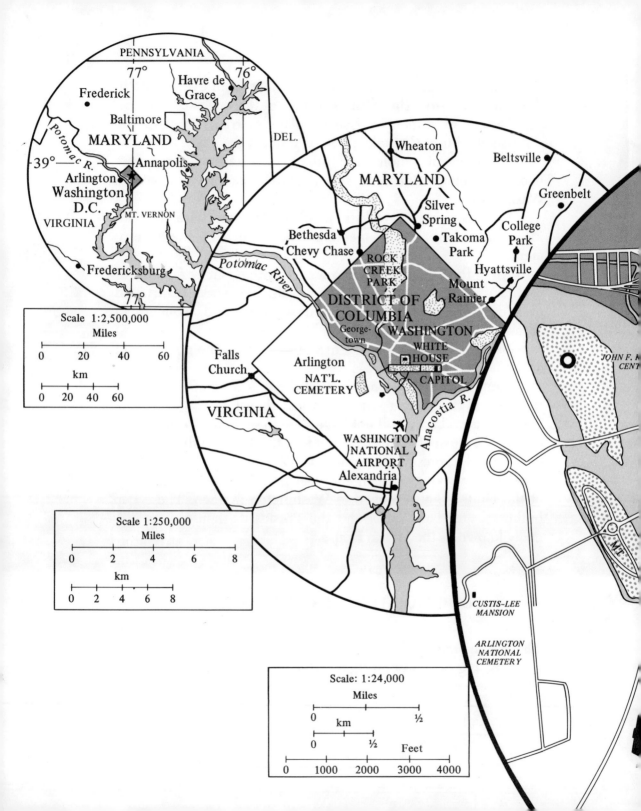

PENNSYLVANIA

77°

76°

Frederick

Havre de
Grace

Baltimore

DEL.

MARYLAND

39°

Potomac R.

Annapolis

Arlington
Washington
D.C.

VIRGINIA

MT. VERNON

77°

Fredericksburg

Scale 1:2,500,000

Miles

0   20   40   60

km

0   20   40   60

Wheaton

Beltsville

MARYLAND

Greenbelt

Silver
Spring

College
Park

Bethesda
Chevy Chase

Takoma
Park

Hyattsville

Potomac River

ROCK
CREEK
PARK

Mount
Rainier

DISTRICT OF
COLUMBIA

George-
town

WASHINGTON

WHITE
HOUSE

Falls
Church

Arlington
NAT'L.
CEMETERY

CAPITOL

JOHN F. K
CENT

VIRGINIA

Anacostia R.

WASHINGTON
NATIONAL
AIRPORT

Alexandria

Scale 1:250,000

Miles

0   2   4   6   8

km

0   2   4   6   8

MT.

CUSTIS–LEE
MANSION

ARLINGTON
NATIONAL
CEMETERY

Scale: 1:24,000

Miles

0   ½

km

0   ½

Feet

0   1000   2000   3000   4000

THREE VIEWS OF WASHINGTON, D.C.

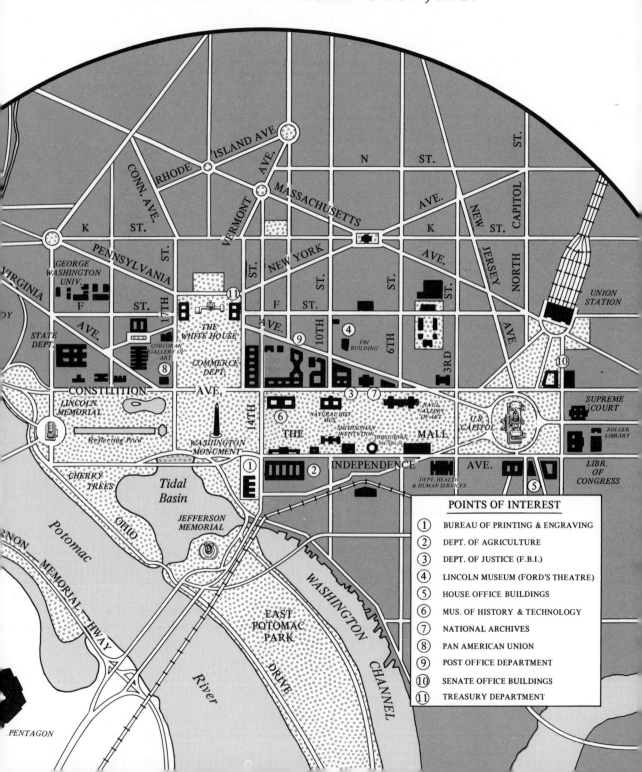

POINTS OF INTEREST

1. BUREAU OF PRINTING & ENGRAVING
2. DEPT. OF AGRICULTURE
3. DEPT. OF JUSTICE (F.B.I.)
4. LINCOLN MUSEUM (FORD'S THEATRE)
5. HOUSE OFFICE BUILDINGS
6. MUS. OF HISTORY & TECHNOLOGY
7. NATIONAL ARCHIVES
8. PAN AMERICAN UNION
9. POST OFFICE DEPARTMENT
10. SENATE OFFICE BUILDINGS
11. TREASURY DEPARTMENT

its tall, white columns, faces Pennsylvania Avenue and gives it its official address—1600 Pennsylvania Avenue. This entrance is used only by special friends of the President and his family, and by state visitors. The President stands on the north porch, for example, to greet a president of another country, or a king or queen arriving at the White House on an official visit.

The door on the opposite side of the house—the south door, behind its lovely curved portico—is used by high government officials and foreign diplomats. When the President gives a dinner for the members of the Supreme Court and their wives, for example, his guests arrive by this door.

The west door is for the special convenience of the President and his staff. They use it as they go back and forth between the White House and the Executive Offices, which are housed in a building west of the White House at the end of an enclosed passage or gallery. The roofs of this gallery, and the similar gallery on the east side of the White House, make pleasant places for the President's family to walk on warm spring evenings, when the magnolias are in bloom.

The east door is the one that could be called the public door. This is the entrance you would use if you arrived at the White House as a tourist, to see it for yourself. You would find the building open to visitors every morning of the year, except Sundays, Mondays, and holidays, from 10 A.M. until noon.

Tourists seldom see the President, or any member of his family. But they can look at the rooms on the first floor of the house, in which important state functions take place.

They see the State Dining Room, and the magnificent gold and white reception hall, called the East Room, where Abigail Adams once hung her laundry.

They also see the three beautiful smaller reception rooms named for the color of their furnishings—the Red Room, the

The White House—
1600 Pennsylvania Avenue

Green Room, and the oval-shaped Blue Room. Grover Cleveland, the only President whose wedding took place in the White House, was married to pretty young Frances Folsom in the Blue Room in 1886.

When the last tourist leaves at 12 noon, a well-trained crew cleans marble floors smudged by hundreds of shoes. Then a long, red rug is unrolled down the length of the first floor hall, from the doorway of the State·Dining Room to the doorway of the East Room. For the rest of the day the White House is once more the private home of the President of the United States.

THIS IS THE WHITE HOUSE

Except for its white-painted outer stone walls, the White House has been completely rebuilt twice during its history.

The first rebuilding took place after the invading British tried to burn the President's house to the ground during the War of 1812. Shortly after it was restored and completely refurnished, the tall, columned porticoes were added to its north and south fronts, giving it the familiar look that all the world knows today.

The many changes made to the inside of the building during the next century added a great deal to the comfort of the Presidents and their families. In 1840, for example, water was first piped into it and forty years later the first two bathrooms were installed.

In 1848, gas pipes brought a new kind of light into every part of the White House except the reception room used by the First Lady, who was then Mrs. James K. Polk. Mrs. Polk knew her friends called her old-fashioned, but she insisted that she preferred candlelight for her room. And those candles were very welcome on the evening the new gas jets were all lit for the first time, for a party—and all unexpectedly went out.

The big, brick kitchen in the basement of the White House got its first stove after Millard Fillmore became President in 1850. The cook immediately complained. Like all the White House cooks before him, he had been preparing state dinners for dozens of guests on open wood fires, and he declared that the new stove did not work. President Fillmore had to go to the Patent Office to study a model of the stove, and learn how to use it himself, before he could convince his cook to try it.

In 1877, Alexander Graham Bell exhibited his new telephone to President Rutherford B. Hayes, and soon the White House had its own telephone. There was a White House phonograph, too, after Thomas A. Edison showed President Hayes his new invention.

Other improvements were made, as time went by, to keep the building up-to-date. Beams had to be drilled and cut away to permit the installation of an ever-growing network of pipes, wires, and ducts. Finally the supporting timbers became seriously weakened. Cracks began to appear in the ceilings. Guests had to be warned not to be frightened by loud noises in the night. Those noises, White House servants explained, were not proof that the house was haunted, but only a sign that it was creaking with age.

By 1949, after thirty-one families had made their home in the White House, architects decided that the 150-year-old building was in danger of collapsing. Its second rebuilding began that year, during the administration of Harry S. Truman. While the work was being done, the President and his family lived across the street, in a residence known as Blair House. (Blair House is now a guest house for the use of the President's offi-

*A delegation of Indians
visiting the White House
during the Civil War.*

cial visitors.) The rebuilding took almost four years and cost close to $6 million.

Today the White House is as strong and solid as experts can make it. It has five elevators, and is fireproofed and air-conditioned. With its central section, its two wings, and the underground areas buried beneath the lawn, it has a total of 132 rooms and twenty baths. Forty-eight of those rooms and fourteen of the baths are in the part of the building used as living quarters by the First Family.

On the roof, where soldiers manned machine guns day and night during World War II, and where President Ulysses S. Grant's young son studied the stars through his telescope, there is now a big, cheerful sunroom.

The old basement kitchen has open fireplaces again, but it is now used for conferences, and for radio and television broadcasts made from the White House. In the new, all-electric kitchen next to it, food is prepared for the big State Dining Room, where more than a hundred people can be seated at dinner, and for the smaller private dining room used by the President and his family when they are not entertaining official guests. The kitchen staff uses a gallon (4 l) of polish each month to keep the White House silver bright and shining.

KEEPING HOUSE AT
1600 PENNSYLVANIA AVENUE

When Abigail Adams first moved into the White House, she said the President could not afford to keep it up on the salary paid to him. Since that time Congress has raised the President's salary. Now Congress also appropriates money for the upkeep of the building, and for the salaries of its staff. Today there are more than eighty people on that staff, including cooks, butlers, maids, gardeners, and maintenance persons.

The man originally sent to the house to install its first electrical wiring was kept on as its official electrician. Later he became the chief usher, in charge of official functions. It was his job to make the arrangements for all guests, and to welcome them when they arrived. He remained at the White House for forty-two years, and knew ten Presidents and their families.

Other members of the staff have stayed at their jobs for a long time too.

One Secret Service man guarded every President from Woodrow Wilson to Franklin Delano Roosevelt, a period of almost thirty years.

One young man hired as a clerk in 1879, and put in charge of the White House mail, stayed at his job for over half a century. At first he handled all the mail himself. But it increased so enormously that before he retired he needed a large staff and a great deal of working space.

The White House mailroom staff keeps a record of all the thousands of letters and packages received every year, but the President himself does not have time to look at everything. Many letters are forwarded to the government department or agency best equipped to answer them.

If a student writes to the President for information about the White House, for example, a mail clerk forwards the letter to the National Park Service of the United States Department of the Interior, which publishes a free leaflet about the White House and its grounds.

All packages addressed to the White House are tested under a fluoroscope, to make certain they do not contain a bomb or some other explosive object. The Secret Service agents are always on hand to remove any parcel that might be dangerous.

[14]

The many gifts of food received by the President are also tested, usually by the laboratory of the Food and Drug Administration, before they go to the White House kitchen or to a hospital or some other institution.

During a Republican administration, the clerks expect to find miniature elephants of all kinds among the mail—carved, painted, made of candy or cake, even embroidered or crocheted. During a Democratic administration, they expect the Democratic symbol, the donkey, to turn up just as often.

The people on the White House staff are always curious about the changes that will be made when one Presidential administration ends and another one begins.

The wealthy New York lawyer, Chester A. Arthur, for example, startled his staff very much when he became President in 1881. He said immediately that he would not stay in the White House for a single night until it was completely redecorated. And he did not. He lived in the home of a friend while the rooms were being done over, and appeared each evening only to superintend the changes he wanted. He picked out dozens of pieces of furniture that he said were too ugly to keep, and had them carted away to be sold at a public auction. They filled twenty-four big wagons.

In 1961 the wife of President John F. Kennedy had her own ideas about redecorating the White House. She wanted its public rooms to look as much as possible the way they had looked when the building was new. So she acquired a great deal of furniture and decorations of the early 1800s, and this aroused wide public interest in the building's history. Soon afterward a law was passed prohibiting any more auctions of White House property, and in 1964 President Lyndon Johnson created the position of curator of the White House. The White House curator has helped make the building a museum as well as a residence.

[15]

SOUVENIRS OF THE FIRST FAMILIES

Visitors to the White House today can find some reminder of almost every family that has lived there.

In the upstairs room where Abraham Lincoln signed his Emancipation Proclamation stands his extra-long bed. The cover on it was crocheted by Mrs. Calvin Coolidge, wife of the thirtieth President, as her gift to the White House.

At state dinners the big table is sometimes decorated with the centerpiece ordered from Paris by James Monroe, who was the American minister to France before he became President in 1817. It is a large, flat mirror, more than 13 feet (4 m) long, surrounded by small, gilded figures that can hold candles or flowers.

Beneath the west terrace is a swimming pool built for President Franklin D. Roosevelt, who was crippled by poliomyelitis. When his doctor said he needed regular exercise, the American people contributed the money that paid for it. The pool was covered over with a floor by President Richard M. Nixon, who turned the space into a press room for the small army of news men and women regularly covering the activities of the White House.

Here and there, all over the house, are portraits and carved busts of many of the Presidents and their wives. One of the most famous is a big painting of the only President who never lived in the White House—George Washington.

That picture was hanging in the East Room, where it hangs today, when British soldiers marched toward Washington during the War of 1812. Dolley Madison, wife of the fourth President, James Madison, was almost alone in the house at the time. Friends warned her to leave immediately. She filled a trunk with important government papers, which she planned to carry to safety in Virginia. Then she said she also wanted to take Washington's portrait to a safe place.

The big picture frame was screwed to the wall. The friend and servant who remained with Mrs. Madison said it could not be removed.

"I will not leave without it," Dolley Madison declared.

Finally the two men cut the picture out of its frame, and Dolley Madison drove off with it just in time to escape the British invaders who were pouring into the city.

The redcoats who burned the White House that night also smashed and looted most of its furnishings. One soldier carried off President Madison's little wooden medicine chest, filled with bottles of herbs. It remained in the soldier's family for many generations, until a Canadian descendant sent it to President Franklin Roosevelt as a gift. The little bottles still held the dried herbs that Dolley Madison had put into them almost 150 years earlier.

THE WHITE HOUSE LAWN

The public is not generally permitted to stroll around the 18 acres (7.3 hectares) of lawns and gardens that surround the White House, but the carefully guarded grounds are open to visitors on special occasions.

One of those occasions occurs on the day after Easter Sunday. Then children, and grownups who are accompanied by children, are admitted to the grounds for the famous Easter Monday egg-rolling. President Kennedy's young children, Caroline and John, watched from the White House portico as hun-

dreds of boys and girls rolled brightly colored eggs down the gentle slopes. So, years later, did President Jimmy Carter's daughter Amy.

Every spring the grounds are also opened to thousands of visitors for a springtime garden tour, a tradition begun by Mrs. Nixon.

Probably the best-known garden on the grounds is the one called the Rose Garden, just outside the President's Oval Office. President John Adams once planted peas and cabbages there. It didn't become a real Rose Garden until 1913, when the first wife of President Woodrow Wilson planted it with bushes brought from the Wilsons' home in Princeton, N.J. In this beautiful and peaceful garden every President since Kennedy has entertained visitors, held news conferences, and pinned medals on Americans their country wished to honor.

A beautiful magnolia tree, not far from the Rose Garden, was planted by Andrew Jackson. That gruff, plain-spoken man had brought it from his home in Tennessee as a memorial to his wife, Rachel, who died immediately after he was elected President.

President John Quincy Adams, son of Abigail and John Adams—the only President's son ever elected to the office—brought an elm sapling from the Adams home in Massachusetts and planted it on the White House grounds. Another tree on the great sweep of lawn is a weeping birch planted by Mrs. Calvin Coolidge and dedicated to the mothers of the Presidents.

President Carter's daughter and grandson join Easter festivities on the White House lawn.

The big lawn was used as a pasture during World War I, when the second Mrs. Woodrow Wilson kept sheep there. Her friends made fun of her. But when her eighteen sheep were sheared and their wool was auctioned off, so many people wanted "White House wool" that the little flock earned almost $100,000 for the Red Cross.

President Theodore Roosevelt made a count of the birds he saw on the White House grounds while he was President. Among them were a sparrow hawk and a screech owl, and more common birds such as flickers, catbirds, and redheaded woodpeckers.

There have always been squirrels around the house. President Dwight D. Eisenhower found them a great nuisance when he practiced golf on the lawn.

Thomas Jefferson, who loved wild animals, kept grizzly bears on the White House grounds. They had been brought to him from the Far West by Meriwether Lewis, one of the two men Thomas Jefferson had sent on the famous Lewis and Clark Expedition to the Pacific Coast in 1804.

"Old Whitey," the horse that had carried President Zachary Taylor through many battles of the war with Mexico in 1846–1848, spent his last peaceful years outside the White House. And the pony owned by Theodore Roosevelt's children lived there too. Once, when one of the Roosevelt boys was sick, his brothers secretly took the pony into the house, pushed it into the elevator, and took it up to the invalid's second-floor bedroom as a surprise.

Over the years since the White House was built, most Americans gave little thought as to where their Vice-President lived. They didn't know, or didn't care, that that important elected official had no official residence. But that changed after Vice-President Gerald R. Ford became President, on the resignation of President Nixon. And soon a handsome house on the grounds of the Naval Observatory was remodeled to serve as the Vice-Presidential mansion. When Vice-President and Mrs. Walter Mondale moved into it at the beginning of the Carter administration, they brought the work of many American artists into the house.

CONGRESS IN SESSION

Everybody in Washington knows what it means when a bright beam of light flashes out after dark from the big, white, floodlit dome on top of the Capitol. The light is a signal that Congress is especially busy and is working on into the night.

During daylight hours, a flag flies above the south wing of the building, where the House of Representatives sits, and over the opposite wing, where the Senate sits, to signal that those bodies are meeting.

The flags usually go up at noon and come down about 5 P.M. on the weekdays when Congress is in session. It does not usually meet in August, or during the winter holiday season. If the flags appear at noon during these periods, it means the members of Congress have business on hand which must be finished before their vacation begins.

The senators have their offices in two large Senate Office Buildings, each connected to the Capitol by underground subways. The small open cars that ride the subway rails resemble the ones used in amusement parks. Representatives' offices fill three large buildings called the House Office Buildings. Only the newest one is connected to the Capitol by subway. Visitors are allowed to ride on the subways except when they hear

loud bells ring. At the sound of those bells the subway cars will be filled with members of Congress, hurrying from their offices or committee meetings to cast a vote.

The Senate meets in a handsome, rectangular room with rows of seats on the floor arranged in a semicircle. All Democrats sit to the right of the Vice-President, and all Republicans to the left. The desk in front of each senator's chair, marked with a copper nameplate, holds a small bottle of sand—a reminder of the days before the invention of blotters, when sand was used to dry ink. Some of the desks date back to that period. Daniel Webster carved his name on the desk he used when he served in the Senate more than 150 years ago.

The Vice-President of the United States, as president of the Senate, presides over its meetings, unless he has asked a senator to take his place temporarily. Seated in his high carved chair on the central platform, he calls the Senate to order by banging the stand in front of him with a small gavel without a handle. That gavel has been used since the first Congress of 1789.

On the steps of the central platform, or rostrum, sit the pages, neatly dressed in their blue suits. The Senate's pages, like those in the House of Representatives, are from fourteen to eighteen years old. There are nearly one hundred of these busy young messengers altogether, about evenly divided between boys and girls. They must all attend the Capitol Page School, a high school whose classes begin shortly after 6 A.M., so that they will be over by noon when the pages are due at their jobs.

Situated in a balcony, called the gallery, behind the platform are the reporters who keep the world informed of the

The Capitol dome

events that take place in this room. The rest of the gallery, running all the way around the chamber, is open to the public.

At the other end of the Capitol the Speaker of the House also bangs a gavel to call the House of Representatives to order. Beside the Speaker's chair stands a tall bundle of ebony rods, bound together with bands of silver and topped with an eagle perched on a silver globe. This symbol of authority is called the Mace.

The semicircular rows of seats below the Speaker do not have nameplates. Members of this House sit anywhere they wish but, as in the Senate, Democrats sit to the right of the Speaker and Republicans to the left. Tables near the front of the room are for the use of representatives speaking from notes or using graphs or pictures to illustrate what they are saying.

In the gallery above the Speaker's desk are the tables for the members of the press. On the opposite side of the gallery, between the sections open to the public, are several television cameras. They are used, for example, when both Houses of Congress meet in joint session in this room to hear a message delivered by some visiting foreign dignitary or by the President of the United States.

During joint sessions of Congress, which are always held here, the President of the Senate sits in a chair placed beside the Speaker's chair. Guests speak from a lower level of the platform. Even the President of the United States is a guest in this room, and stands on a level below the Speaker when he addresses Congress.

A joint session of Congress meets in the House of Representatives.

THE CAPITOL AND HOW IT GREW

Washington visitors can get passes from senators or representatives that admit them to the sessions of Congress. Many visitors like to ask for a pass in order to see the office of a congressman and some of the busy people on his staff.

But visitors can also watch Congress at work by joining one of the regular Capitol tours that start every few minutes from the Rotunda, the great central hall of the Capitol roofed by the dome itself.

The statues in this room are of American Presidents. The paintings on the wall and on the great curved ceiling, 180 feet (55 m) above the floor, illustrate important events in American history. One of the paintings on the lower part of the wall, the one called *The Signing of the Declaration of Independence*, has been copied so many times that most visitors are already familiar with it. The artist, John Trumbull, was the friend of many of the men in that painting, and an aide to General Washington during the Revolution.

An Italian artist, Constantino Brumidi, painted the huge picture on the inside of the dome, and most of the frescoed panels that encircle the room just below it. Brumidi did not complete all the panels, because he died after a fall from the high scaffold he worked on. Today a gallery runs around the room at the height of Brumidi's scaffold. The stairway that leads to it has 365 steps, one for each day in the year.

The Capitol grew slowly from its small beginnings. A second box-shaped building, a twin to the one where Congress met in 1800, and connected to it by a wooden passageway, was finished before the War of 1812. But on the night the British set fire to the White House, they also burned "this harbor of

Yankee democracy," as they called it. Work on the Capitol had to be started over again, almost from the ground up.

That time, when the two wings were built—one for the Senate, one for the House of Representatives—they were connected by a solid stone structure capped by a low copper-covered dome. Some architects think the Capitol was handsomer then than it has ever been since.

But as more states joined the Union, there were more senators and more representatives and the building became crowded. Finally Congress was so cramped for space that it voted to build a large extension on each side of the Capitol. It also voted to replace the low central dome with a much larger and more impressive one made of cast iron.

The two extensions went up fairly rapidly. By 1857 the representatives moved into the big new hall in the southern extension, where they still meet today. For some time after that their old room was empty. Cobwebs gathered in the corners. Peddlers squatted on the floor selling oranges and gingerbread to sightseers and government clerks.

Finally the congressmen, ashamed of their bad housekeeping, had their old room cleaned out and dedicated it as a National Statuary Hall. They asked each state to contribute to the Hall the statues of two of its distinguished citizens. The states responded so eagerly that the room could not hold all the statues. Some of them had to be placed in other parts of the building.

American visitors to the Statuary Hall today like to look for the statues sent by their own states. They also like to experiment with a trick discovered by John Quincy Adams. If they stand at a certain spot on the floor, marked by a brass plate, and speak in a whisper, they can be heard on the far side of the room.

The northern extension of the Capitol was completed in

*Statuary Hall in the old
House of Representatives wing*

1859, and the Senate then moved into the big chamber it has occupied ever since. The old Senate room became, for a time, the chamber of the Supreme Court.

Work started on the big new dome at the same time the extensions were begun. But the dome was still far from finished when Lincoln became President in 1861. He took his oath of office on the Capitol's east steps, where most American Presidents have been inaugurated. And many people, looking up at the headless Capitol behind him, thought it might be a symbol. Several Southern states had already seceded from the Union. A civil war seemed inevitable. If the federal government were defeated, its Capitol might be destroyed before it had been completed. The ugly wooden scaffold for workmen, around the base of the dome, made the building look as if it were already being attacked.

Within a few months the Civil War actually did begin. Southern armies, just across the Potomac in Virginia, threatened the city of Washington. Weary Union soldiers practiced marching on the Capitol lawn and slept on the floor of the Rotunda.

But above the soldiers' heads, as they slept, men were still laboring on the big dome. Lincoln had ordered the work to continue. He had told the people of the United States that the Union would be saved. He was proving the strength of his own faith in the Union by finishing its Capitol.

On December 2, 1863, the last stone column and the last segment of the dome were in place. A cheering crowd gathered to watch the 19-foot (5.8-m) bronze Statue of Freedom hoisted into its place above the completed dome. "The Capitol is finally finished," people said.

But the Capitol wasn't really finished. In 1958 work began on another enlargement. The east wall of the central section was

*Abraham Lincoln rides to the
unfinished Capitol for his
inauguration on March 4, 1861.*

pushed outward about 30 feet (9 m), to make still more room inside. So long as the country continues to grow, the Capitol may also go on growing. Someday it may even be abandoned, as too small or inconvenient for the needs of future members of Congress. But any new building in which Congress may someday meet will probably be called the Capitol.

THE SUPREME COURT

At ten o'clock on certain weekdays another gavel bangs in a handsome white marble building opposite the Capitol. In that building sit the nine justices of the Supreme Court, the highest court in the land.

Even before the gavel sounds, the room in which the Court meets is hushed and quiet. The long table for the justices, called the bench, and the nine empty chairs behind it, stand against a sober background of deep red curtains. In front of the table, lawyers are studying the papers spread out before them. The quill pens on their desks, like the bottles of sand on the desks of senators, are a reminder that the Supreme Court is an ancient body, as old as the Constitution of the United States. According to the Constitution, this Court, and the other federal courts that work under it, form the judiciary branch of the government. It is equal in power and authority to the other two branches, the legislative and the executive.

There are visitors present, in the rows of seats separated from the front part of the room by an iron railing. Even the visitors speak quietly. The Supreme Court is about to open. It is a solemn moment.

At the sound of the gavel everyone in the room rises. Messengers draw apart the red curtains, and through the opening come the nine justices. They are wearing long black robes. They take their places silently in the nine chairs. The Chief Justice sits in the middle.

Then the clerk of the Court announces that the Court is open. He bangs the gavel again, and everyone sits down. The first case is called.

There is no jury in the Supreme Court. The nine justices listen to the opposing lawyers and each makes his decision. Most cases they hear have already been tried in a lower court, perhaps in several lower courts. The justices have agreed to review a specific case—that is, to hear the case themselves—in order to give their opinion on the particular point of law involved.

The lawyers who plead the case have already given the justices written statements of their arguments. Therefore, each side is usually allowed only half an hour to speak and to answer any questions the justices may ask. Occasionally the justices may allow a lawyer an hour or even more to present a complicated case.

Later, in private, the justices will spend many more hours studying and discussing each case they have heard. They usually hold court only two weeks out of every four, between October and June. They spend the rest of the time in study and discussion.

If they all come to the same decision on a case, the Chief Justice appoints a justice to write the opinion (or decision) for the whole Court. If they disagree, the Chief Justice appoints

*The main entrance to
the Supreme Court Building*

two justices—one to write the opinion of the majority of the Court members, one to write the opinion of the minority. Any justice who disagrees with the written opinion may write one of his own. All opinions are made public.

The Supreme Court Building has been called beautiful, majestic, and magnificent. And most visitors agree that it is a fitting home for the important work that goes on in it. Most of that work, of course, is done in parts of the building closed to the public. Each justice, for example, has his own private suite of offices which he shares with his two law clerks, a secretary and a messenger. In the building there is also a law library and conference room that the public never sees. When the justices hold their regular meetings in that conference room, not even their law clerks may enter it. The youngest justice, in terms of time on the Court, opens the door when anyone knocks during a meeting, takes delivery of a message or a book some justice has sent for, and then closes the door securely again.

Visitors enter the building through the main entrance, past the tall marble columns and under these words carved in stone: EQUAL JUSTICE UNDER LAW. They may look through open doors into the courtroom, if court is not in session. They may wander along corridors lined with paintings and statues of former justices, and documents that are part of the Court's history. They may admire the building's two famous spiral staircases, each elliptical in shape and twisting its way upward for five stories without any visible center support. They may eat in the building's cafeteria. But if they hope to see one of the justices there, they are usually disappointed. The justices have their own private dining room.

THE BIRTH OF A CAPITAL

During the autumn of 1790—just ten years before Abigail Adams moved into the President's house overlooking the Potomac—George Washington was riding along the banks of that river. He had been elected the first President of the United States only a few months before, and he was carrying out one of the first duties of his office. At the request of Congress, he was choosing the site for a national capital.

The congressmen—all members of Congress at the time, and for many years afterward, were men—had argued for a long time about the location of the capital. At first they planned to choose a city that was already important, and make it the seat of the federal government. Some wanted Philadelphia, the temporary capital, to become the permanent one. Men from other parts of the country wanted a city in their own state to be chosen. New Yorkers wanted New York to be the capital. The people of Maryland wanted the capital to be Baltimore.

"We will make many enemies no matter which city we choose," a congressman said finally. "So let us build a completely new town for our national capital."

It was a daring idea. No government had ever done such a thing. (The governments of three nations—Australia, India, and Brazil—have adopted the idea since 1900.) But the congressmen were not afraid of new ideas. They agreed to build a new "federal town." It would stand on land that belonged to the federal government, and it would be governed by the government of the United States.

The next thing the congressmen had to decide was the location of the new town. Northerners wanted it in the North. Southerners wanted it in the South.

At the same time, of course, the congressmen and the first President had other problems to solve. One of the most important was: Should each state repay out of its own Treasury the money it had borrowed during the Revolution for the support of its own troops? Or should Congress adopt the plan suggested by Alexander Hamilton, Secretary of the Treasury, and pay all those state debts out of the national Treasury?

Most Northerners were in favor of Hamilton's plan. They knew it would increase the strength of the federal government, and they were in favor of a national government stronger than the governments of the individual states.

Most Southerners, including Thomas Jefferson of Virginia, were opposed to Hamilton's scheme. They did not want the federal government to be stronger than the state governments. The arguments went on and on.

One day Hamilton made a suggestion to Jefferson. He offered to persuade certain Northern congressmen to vote for building the new federal capital in the South—if Jefferson would persuade certain Southern congressmen to vote for Hamilton's debt plan.

And so it was worked out. Congress voted for Hamilton's plan, and also voted to build the capital on the banks of the Potomac. That compromise settled the location of the new federal city.

Then Congress asked President Washington, who lived along the Potomac, to choose the area that would be named the District of Columbia, in honor of Christopher Columbus. The nation's new capital would be built inside that district.

George Washington
in a painting by Rembrandt Peale

The 100 square miles (259 sq km) President Washington selected were partly in Virginia but mostly in Maryland. The two small colonial villages of Alexandria and Georgetown were inside it. Both Virginia and Maryland agreed to turn over to the federal government their rights to the land. (Years later the Virginia section, including the town of Alexandria, was returned to that state. That is why the District of Columbia is no longer square and covers only 69 square miles [179 sq km].)

President Washington then asked the nineteen property owners in the new district to give the federal government enough land for the capital city's streets. He also asked them to sell to the government, for about $65 an acre, the land that would be needed for a President's house, a Capitol, and other federal buildings.

The property owners agreed because they thought the rest of their land would increase in value when it became part of the capital city of the United States. They planned to cut the land up into lots and sell them at high prices for homes, stores, hotels, and other businesses. Land along the water, President Washington told them, was sure to be especially valuable. He was certain the new city would soon become a rich and busy port.

Then President Washington sent for Major Pierre Charles L'Enfant, the handsome young engineer he had chosen to plan the new city.

L'ENFANT AND HIS PLAN

L'Enfant was a Frenchman who had followed Lafayette across the Atlantic during the Revolution to fight on the side of the American colonies. After the war, he remained in the United

States because he had great confidence in its future. When he heard that Congress had decided to build a new federal capital, he wrote to President Washington to say he would be very proud if he might help create a capital city that would be "magnificent enough to grace a great nation."

Soon L'Enfant was conferring with President Washington in the village of Georgetown. The little stone cottage where they are said to have met is still standing. Washington gave the engineer only one suggestion. He told L'Enfant where he thought the President's house should stand, at the heart of the new capital, which was to be built north of Alexandria and east of Georgetown.

Then L'Enfant began to ride up and down along the banks of the Potomac. With him were two American surveyors—Andrew Ellicott of Maryland, and Ellicott's tall friend, Benjamin Banneker, a free black man.

L'Enfant first chose the location of the Capitol—on top of a little rise then called Jenkins' Hill. The Capitol, he decided, would be the central point of a checkerboard of streets filling the whole triangle of land formed by the Potomac and one of its branches, the Anacostia.

But a simple checkerboard of streets did not satisfy the Frenchman's idea of a grand city. He also planned many magnificent avenues, each 160 feet (48.7 m) wide, extending out from certain points like wheel spokes. They would be useful, he said, because they would connect one part of the city with another by the most direct route.

The street connecting the President's house and the Capitol, L'Enfant thought, should be the finest in the city. Today, that street, part of Pennsylvania Avenue, is probably the most famous mile (1.6 km) of roadway in America. Along it have passed the inaugural parades of every President since Jefferson,

and the funeral processions of Presidents who have died in office. Here the city of Washington stages great parades to honor its heroes and its most distinguished visitors.

Beautiful parks, where Americans could build fountains and put up statues, were on L'Enfant's plan too. Wherever three or more streets met, he planned a parklike square. He also planned a garden-bordered parkway, 400 feet (122 m) wide, running westward from the Capitol along a marshy stream. Today, that stream no longer exists, but the parkway L'Enfant dreamed of is Washington's great Mall. The Washington Monument stands part way along this sweep of tree-bordered grass. The Lincoln Memorial stands at the far-western end. The shimmering water of a long pool, between them, reflects America's tributes to two of its greatest Presidents.

L'Enfant and his plan caused a lot of trouble. The property owners of the district agreed to give land for the capital city's streets, but they thought a strip of land about 50 feet (15.3 m) wide was enough for the most important thoroughfare. They were horrified when L'Enfant told them how much free land the government would need to lay out the broad streets he had designed. They complained to President Washington.

Then one rich property owner started to build a house not far from Jenkins' Hill. L'Enfant told him to tear it down, because it would be in the way of one of the city's avenues. And when the owner laughed at him, L'Enfant ordered workmen to destroy the house.

*The funeral procession
of Franklin D. Roosevelt
on April 14, 1945*

Finally President Washington received so many complaints about L'Enfant that he had to dismiss him. Congress offered the French engineer payment for his two years of work, which L'Enfant refused. But when he left he took his plan with him.

President Washington and the members of his government did not know what to do. They wanted to start building the capital, but they had no plan for it.

Then something surprising happened. Benjamin Banneker offered to draw the L'Enfant plan from memory.

People had noticed the tall black man striding along the riverbank with L'Enfant and Ellicott, the surveyor. Most of them thought Banneker was Ellicott's servant. They did not think Banneker could even read and write. They were sure a black man could not know anything about surveying or planning a city.

They were wrong. Banneker was an educated man. He owned a fine farm and was an excellent farmer. He had taught himself mathematics and astronomy and other branches of science. Later he published almanacs, full of accurate information about the stars and the tides. And he had a remarkable memory. Soon he had completed a copy of the L'Enfant plan for the new city.

On September 18, 1793, President Washington came to the District of Columbia to lay the cornerstone of the north wing of the Capitol. He hoped the building would soon be completed, and that wealthy businessmen would soon be helping to create a handsome national capital.

THE CAPITAL GROWS UP

The new federal city did not become a port, as George Washington believed it would. From the time the government moved there in 1800, the city's only real business was the business of government. And for many years the government of the United States was weak and poor. This was partly because the country was still young and struggling and had many enemies. And it was partly because many people still wanted the state governments to be stronger than the national government. So the new federal capital did not become a big, handsome city right away.

Even when it grew larger, it did not become the magnificent city L'Enfant had dreamed of. This was because Congress, which governed it, was not interested in spending money to improve it.

Both houses of Congress had appointed committees to look after the affairs of Washington and the District of Columbia. These men, like most elected representatives, were careful to look out for the best interests of the voters in their own states. They knew that if they failed in this task, they would probably not be reelected. But since the committee members were not afraid of angering the voteless people who lived in the District of Columbia, they were generally content to appropriate only enough funds to keep the District bumbling along.

The Washingtonians, of course, complained bitterly about this offhand treatment. But they had no congressmen of their own to fight their battles for them. "We pay taxes to the federal government," they said, "but we have no representation. That is 'taxation without representation'—the very thing Americans fought against in the Revolution." But Congress would not change the laws that gave it control over the national capital.

Each year more people came to live in Washington. They needed homes, hotels, and shops. But most of the men who were willing to invest in Washington business enterprises cared very little about making their national capital a beautiful place. They cared only about making money as fast as possible. And Congress did nothing to control or regulate their money-making schemes. So the speculators built cheaply on whatever land they could buy for the lowest prices. The business centers that grew up here and there were not arranged according to any plan. And if the buildings did not show a large profit, they were neglected and allowed to fall into ruin.

Some of L'Enfant's avenues were laid out, each one named for a state in the Union. But even before L'Enfant died in 1825, poor and forgotten, his great plan had been almost forgotten too.

When the first railroad reached Washington in 1835, its tracks came right up to the foot of Capitol Hill. Some Washingtonians objected, saying that this destroyed the dignity of the Capitol. But Congress allowed the tracks to remain.

The Civil War brought a huge new population to the city. Soldiers tramped through the mud of unpaved Pennsylvania Avenue, and built barracks alongside it. Thousands of blacks, fleeing slave-owners in the South, crowded into miserable shacks along the narrow alleys cut between Washington's streets. The "get-rich-quick" builders who put up those shacks gave Washington its first real slums. Capitol Hill, a visitor said, was "dreary, desolate, and dirty."

But the Civil War proved to be an important turning point in the history of the city. The defeat of the Confederacy was

Union armies on review

[44]

the defeat of people who believed in powerful state governments. The victory of the Union was the victory of people who believed in a strong federal government. After the war, for the first time, all Americans looked to Washington, the federal capital, as the real heart of the United States.

That is why other congressmen finally agreed when, in 1901, Senator James McMillan of Michigan said something should be done to improve the city. They asked the advice of a group of architects and park commissioners on the best way to make Washington a capital worthy of a great nation.

The group said, in effect, "Remodel Washington according to the forgotten plan of the French engineer L'Enfant."

Congress took their advice. The long, slow job of remodeling the 100-year-old city began.

Soon the railroad tracks at the foot of Capitol Hill disappeared. The first step had been taken toward creating the green Mall that reminds us today of the garden-bordered parkway L'Enfant had imagined for that place. Now another great, green stretch of park, running from the White House to the Potomac, crosses the Mall to form a huge cross, with the Washington Monument at its center.

During the First and Second World Wars, many flimsy temporary structures had to be put up to take care of the thousands of new workers who had flooded into Washington. Those structures were not replaced overnight. But since the early days of the twentieth century, all new permanent government buildings, monuments, and statues must be approved by special planning commissions who still use the French engineer's plan as their guide.

The shameful alley slums are being cleared away. Decayed old structures are being rebuilt or torn down to make way for new ones. Now there are many magnificent white marble buildings in the city, many handsome, tree-lined avenues and lovely green parks, just as George Washington and the young French engineer dreamed of long ago.

The passage of time also brought changes in the way the District of Columbia is governed. In 1961 the Twenty-third Amendment to the Constitution gave Washington residents the right to vote for the nation's President and Vice-President. In 1970 Congress granted the District one delegate to the House of Representatives, but that delegate may not vote with the other representatives on the floor of the House. Today District residents elect their own mayor and a thirteen-member council, and have won the right to levy taxes to carry on the business of their city government. But Congress has kept the right to veto, or block, the council's actions.

GETTING AROUND IN WASHINGTON

Visitors often get lost in Washington, but the people who live here say that it is easy to get around in the city.

The first thing to remember, they say, is that Washington is divided into sections by two lines which cross at the Capitol. One line runs north and south. (It is formed by North Capitol Street and South Capitol Street.) The other line runs east and west. (It is formed by East Capitol Street and the Mall.)

The names of the four sections divided by these lines are Northwest, Northeast, Southwest, and Southeast, abbreviated as NW, NE, SW, and SE.

Over: the Capitol Building

If Washingtonians want to tell you where they live, or work, they always mention the section their home or office is in.

"You can find my office easily," they may say. "It's at the corner of D and 7th streets, Northwest."

One of the city's four sections, the Northwest, is far larger than the others. It is in this section that visitors do most of their sightseeing, because so many important buildings are there. Usually they can find the building they want to visit on one of the maps of this area especially printed to help visitors find their way around the city.

The White House is in the Northwest section. So are many of the buildings where the various bureaus and agencies of the federal government carry on their work.

THEY WORK FOR THE GOVERNMENT

Most people who work for the federal government in Washington are Civil Service employees.

The Civil Service is a system for choosing government employees on merit—that is, for their knowledge and skill and ability to do a certain kind of work. These qualities are tested by examinations that may be taken by men and women in every state and territory of the Union. Jobs are given to the applicants with the best examination grades. (Not all Civil Service employees work in Washington, of course. Letter carriers all over the country, for example, are also Civil Service employees.)

Some Civil Service workers, and other government specialists who do not come under the Civil Service regulations, work in Washington for only a year or two at a time. People who work for the State Department, for example, may take their training in Washington and then leave for some distant land to serve in an American embassy or consulate. After several years, they may return to Washington for a time, and then once more leave for a foreign country. Armed Forces personnel come and go too. So do many people who work for the Department of Agriculture and other government agencies.

Most government employees work in offices or laboratories that visitors never see. But in many federal buildings the public is invited to look behind the scenes at the people who work there, or to study exhibits that have been arranged to illustrate the program of a certain government agency or department.

In the lobby of the Department of Commerce building, for example, visitors can watch a big board on which flashing colored lights tell the story of America's population growth from minute to minute. Each time the blue light flashes it means that a baby has been born in the United States. The flashing purple light means that a death has occurred. The flashing green light means that an immigrant has arrived in the United States from some foreign country. And the white light that flashes on several times each minute shows that the country's population is increasing at the rate of one person for each flash. The timing of the flashing lights is changed when a new census is taken. The blue light flashes oftener each minute, for example, when the birth rate increases.

In the basement of the building is the National Aquarium—the oldest aquarium in the nation. Here, collected by employees of the U.S. Fish and Wildlife Service, are electric eels, sharks, turtles, brilliant tropical fish, ornamental carp from Japan, and dozens of other varieties of water life, swimming or crawling about in some sixty big tanks. The aquarium is known especially for its vast collection of fish native to the United States.

Visitors to the J. Edgar Hoover Building can learn there

exactly how crimes are solved by the FBI—the Federal Bureau of Investigation. They see the huge fingerprint file, and may have their own fingerprints taken. They look into the ballistics laboratory where a gun can be tested and matched to the bullet found at the scene of a crime. They see the serology laboratory where blood is tested, and other laboratories where experts test samples of hair, cloth, leather, and other substances. They learn how shoeprints and tiremarks can be used to catch criminals, and how an expert can prove that the signature on a check has been forged. Their tour ends with a visit to the target pistol range where, from behind bulletproof glass, they may see an exhibition of rapid-fire marksmanship.

Visitors are also welcome at the broadcasting studios of the Voice of America in the building of what was long called the Department of Health, Education and Welfare, and is now called the Department of Health and Human Services. Day and night Voice of America broadcasters send out radio programs in thirty-six languages. They give news reports, conduct interviews, and play music. All around the world people can learn how Americans work and play and live by listening to these broadcasts.

The Treasury Building, third oldest federal building in the city, is next to the White House. People are often puzzled by its location because it prevents the White House and the Capitol from being in perfect sight of each other. Legend says President Jackson was responsible for where it stands. After listening impatiently to long arguments among members of Congress as to

Coin collectors wait outside the Treasury Building to buy a new issue.

[52]

where a Treasury should be built, it is said Jackson finally stamped out of the White House, crossed the east lawn and jabbed his cane into the ground. "Put it here!" he said.

In the Treasury Building, an exhibit showing the work of the Coast Guard reminds visitors that Alexander Hamilton founded this branch of the service in 1790, when he was Secretary of the Treasury. In order to collect customs for foreign goods entering American ports, he asked Congress to give him ten small sailing vessels called cutters. Those custom-collecting boats gradually increased in number, and began to do other work as well—such as maintaining lighthouses and carrying out rescue missions on the high seas. During wartime the Coast Guard becomes an arm of the navy. But during peacetime it is still administered by the United States Treasury.

In the Post Office Department Building is an exhibit of all the postage stamps issued by the United States. Many philatelists, or stamp collectors, visit this exhibit every day. They can also buy stamps here for their own collections. All United States stamps are printed at the Bureau of Engraving and Printing, where United States money is also printed.

MONEY, MONEY EVERYWHERE

Visitors to the Bureau of Engraving and Printing walk along narrow galleries high above the rooms where stamps and paper money are printed. The visitors can look down on stacks of hundred-dollar bills, but they can never get close enough to touch them. Every part of this building is well guarded. The tons of special paper used here are kept in vaults. The inks used here are made from secret formulas.

Paper bills are printed thirty-two at a time, on big sheets, on printing presses that print 150 sheets per minute. The sheets are counted many times during the printing process. They are also carefully examined under bright lights. If there is an oil spot, or any other imperfection on a sheet, the whole sheet is discarded and destroyed. The perfect sheets are finally cut up into separate bills, counted again, and bound in packages of 100 each. The value of the paper money printed here each year is about $20 billion.

About 12 million bills of various denominations are turned out each day, most of them dollar bills. A dollar bill usually lasts about thirteen months before it becomes too worn out to keep in circulation. When it is turned in for a new bill, it is burned in a special incinerator. Millions of dollars worth of bills are burned every day.

The bureau also prints government savings bonds, invitations for official White House receptions, and other items. More than three thousand people work in the Bureau of Engraving and Printing, and more than half of them are women.

THREE PRECIOUS DOCUMENTS

The National Archives Building stands in the triangle of land between Pennsylvania and Constitution avenues, Northwest. Like most of the other structures in this Federal Triangle, as it is called, the National Archives was built in the twentieth century. It was finished in 1935. The windowless building is faced by 72 stone columns, each weighing 95 tons (86 mt). Its bronze doors, said to be the largest in the world, are 1 foot (.3 m) thick and 40 feet (12 m) high.

Visitors to this building usually do not see the experts and scholars who work here, studying and preserving the important papers of the federal government and other vital records. Among those records are millions of maps, charts, and aerial photographs. There are also the passenger lists of crowded ships that carried European immigrants to the United States, and lists of the people brought by slave ships to this country from Africa. In the National Archives there are over 80,000 reels of motion picture film, going back to the 1897 inauguration of President William McKinley. And there are billions of pages of manuscripts—enough to fill 250,000 filing cabinets. Every year thousands of people consult this material for the writing of books and articles, or for tracing their families back to their earliest roots in America.

Most visitors come to see just three documents that are on exhibit here—the three most valuable documents in the United States. They are the original Declaration of Independence, the Constitution, and the Constitution's first ten amendments, known as the Bill of Rights.

During the War of 1812, a frightened State Department clerk discovered that these precious documents had been left behind when the government fled Washington just ahead of the British invaders. He hastily stuffed them into linen bags, found a wagon, and carted the documents off to safety in Virginia.

Today, these documents are as safe as science can make them. They are sealed in bronze and glass cases filled with

Visitors study the Declaration of Independence, the Constitution, and the Bill of Rights on display in the National Archives.

THE
DECLARATION OF INDEPENDENCE
AND THE
CONSTITUTION
OF THE
UNITED STATES OF AMERICA

helium gas (instead of air) to protect them from the harmful effects of oxygen. Special filters shut out any light rays which may be harmful. A guard stands on watch beside the cases all day.

Beneath those cases, under a marble floor, is a remarkable vault built especially to safeguard the documents in case of an emergency. It is burglarproof, fireproof, and shockproof. The cases holding the documents can be lowered into this vault at an instant's notice. The elevator that carries them down is electrically operated. If the electric power were cut off, the elevator would function just as quickly on its storage batteries, which are always ready to take over if necessary.

Visitors can see how this amazing device works by studying a small model of it. Every few minutes during the day, the tiny glass cases in the model disappear as if by magic into the small vault beneath them.

THE LIBRARY OF CONGRESS

Although the Library of Congress was originally founded for the exclusive use of congressmen, today its collections are available to other government workers, to libraries (through an interlibrary loan service), to scholars, and to the general public.

A member of Congress doesn't even have to go to the Library of Congress to get one of its volumes. When an order is telephoned to the library, the book is quickly sent to the Capitol through an underground tube like a miniature subway. Members of Congress can also obtain information on almost any subject by telephoning the library's Congressional Research Service. That service receives about 300,000 requests for information each year.

Everyone is welcome to visit this amazing storehouse of information and study its collections of books, newspapers, manuscripts, and other items. The size of these collections is staggering. Over 70 million items are stored in the library's three buildings, and the number grows by about 7,000 a day. There are, for example, some 18 million books on its 350 miles (563 km) of shelves. About two-thirds of those books are written in one of the 470 foreign languages that may be read here.

The library has 4 million pieces of music, ranging from ancient handwritten religious music to modern jazz and rock. Visitors can listen to concerts played on valuable old instruments the library owns. Tape recordings of these concerts are lent to colleges and other educational institutions.

The Main Reading Room is in the oldest building, built in 1897, and is one of the first things visitors see. It is octagonal in shape and its ceiling is the building's dome 160 feet (48.7 m) above the floor. In the center is the librarians' circular desk, and around it in concentric circles are desks for 212 readers and researchers. There are 44,000 reference books in this one room alone along with part of the main catalog which consists of 20 million catalog cards. A computerized retrieval system helps researchers find the information they seek.

Most visitors want especially to see the library's most famous treasures. One of them is Lincoln's own handwritten copy

Over: the Main Reading Room
of the Library of Congress

[59]

of the Gettysburg Address—the paper he read from as he made his famous speech on the Civil War battlefield. Another is an early version of the Declaration of Independence. This copy was written by Thomas Jefferson, but visitors who look closely can see that certain words here and there were crossed out. The new words written in, to take their place, are in the handwriting of John Adams and Benjamin Franklin.

A single librarian looked after the Library of Congress when it was first started in a room in the Capitol. Then there were fewer than a thousand books on its shelves. Today several thousand people make up the library's staff, including about 800 who work in the Congressional Research Service.

About 500,000 books, pieces of music, and other creative items that the library receives each year are given to it. American publishers send to the library two copies of each new work they publish, along with a small fee. They do this in order to obtain a copyright, which is rather like the patent an inventor obtains by sending the Patent Office the plans for a new invention.

On the back of the title page of this book, for example, you will see the words *Copyright © 1961, 1981 by Franklin Watts, Inc.* This copyright notice, as it is called, tells you that if anyone other than Franklin Watts, Inc., wishes to publish and sell copies of this book, he or she must get permission from the copyright owner, Franklin Watts, Inc.

With the copyright notice, usually on the back of the title page, you will also see the number 80–25022. This is the number by which librarians can order a copy of the book's catalog card filed in the Library of Congress. The card lists the name of the book, the names of its authors, artist, and publisher, the date and place of its publication, its size, and table of contents.

Copies of this card are sold to libraries all over the country. The file cards for many of the books in your own library may have been purchased from the Library of Congress.

The Library of Congress is still a branch of the federal government. Today, however, it also belongs to the nation, and serves the whole world.

STOREHOUSES OF TREASURE

The Library of Congress is not the only treasure storehouse in the nation's capital.

A remarkable collection of things owned and used by President Abraham Lincoln, for example, is kept in the building where Lincoln was assassinated on the night of April 14, 1865. The building was then Ford's Theater, and Lincoln had come to see a play called *Our American Cousin.* He was sitting quietly in his box watching the performance when the actor John Wilkes Booth entered the box and shot him from behind. Afterward the theater seats were ripped out, and the building was made into a Lincoln Museum. But in 1964 Congress voted over $2 million to restore the old Ford Theater so that people could see how it looked on the night of the assassination.

Across the street from the museum is the house where Lincoln died the morning after he was shot. He had been carried there by doctors who were afraid to send him over Washington's rough streets to the White House. This house is now a museum too.

Some of the most important museums in Washington were not bought or built by the government. They were put up by men who grew wealthy in the United States and who wanted to share with the American people some of the treasures their wealth had bought.

The great National Gallery of Art, which opened in 1941, was a gift to the nation from Andrew Mellon, a wealthy Pittsburgher who served as Secretary of the Treasury from 1921 to 1932, and as ambassador to Great Britain. Mellon also gave the museum its first 111 paintings, many of them priceless old masterpieces.

The National Gallery was about thirty years old when Mellon's son and daughter and the Mellon Foundation gave the nation the striking new East Building, connected to the original National Gallery by an underground concourse. The East Building, actually a pair of buildings constructed with sharp angular corners, was especially designed by I. M. Pei to fit the triangular plot on which it stands.

Another center of art in Washington is the Hirshhorn Museum and Sculpture Garden, on the south side of the Mall across from the National Gallery of Art. This circular building was the gift of Joseph Hirshhorn, an immigrant from Latvia who made his fortune from uranium mines. The museum opened in 1974 with about 6,000 pieces of contemporary art. Hirshhorn himself collected 2,000 of the sculptures the museum owns.

The Corcoran Gallery of Art was built by a Washington banker, William Corcoran, who wanted to honor American art and encourage American artists. Many visitors here are especially interested in a portrait of George Washington by Gilbert Stuart, who lived and worked during the early years of the nation's history. Probably no other picture in the world has been copied so often. This picture of Washington has appeared on stamps and is on every American dollar bill.

*Marino Marini's "Horse and Rider" statue
outside the Hirshhorn Museum*

The Folger Shakespeare Library is a storehouse of treasures from the time of Shakespeare and England's first Queen Elizabeth—the time when Englishmen were planning their first colonies in America. The theater inside this building, where Shakespeare's plays are performed, is exactly like a theater of Shakespeare's time. The library is named for its founder, Henry Clay Folger, a millionaire oil executive. Together with his wife, he spent most of the last fifty years of his life collecting the valuable books and other objects that are stored here.

THE SMITHSONIAN

The most amazing storehouse of treasures in Washington was a gift to the American people from an English scientist, James Smithson. In his will he left $500,000 to establish the Smithsonian Institution.

No one knows why this scientist chose to leave his money for this purpose. He had never visited the United States. When he died in 1829, the city of Washington was still a muddy village with unpaved streets which, as one English visitor said, "begin in nothing and lead nowhere." At that time, many people in Europe—and many Americans too—were not certain that the United States would continue to exist. But Smithson apparently had great faith in the new nation he had never seen, and he wished to do something to help its people and its capital city. So he left his fortune ($500,000 was a huge fortune in those days) to establish the institution that is now famous all over the world.

There are so many thousands of treasures in the Smithsonian Institution that they fill several large buildings. The

Smithsonian owns something like 75 million objects, and acquires about a million more every year. Only about 2 percent of its vast collections can be shown at any one time, but its staff changes its exhibits constantly. Often an entire hall is remodelled to provide the proper setting for a new display.

One exhibit is a whole house, brought to Washington peg by peg and board by board from Massachusetts, where it was built in 1678. Workmen rebuilt it inside the museum, and now the low-ceilinged parlor and kitchen are furnished just as they might have been when the house was a family home more than three centuries ago.

Suspended from the ceiling of one hall of the Smithsonian hangs the world's first man-carrying, power-driven airplane—the machine invented by the Wright brothers, and flown by them at Kitty Hawk, North Carolina, in 1903. There are early automobiles too, and early sewing machines, steam engines, and models of many other mechanical devices.

There is a famous collection of gems. There are exhibits of wild animals and birds, and of prehistoric animals. In the American Indian Hall there are life-sized groups of Indians with weapons and tools they used in their daily life.

In the First Ladies' Hall visitors can see figures representing all the First Ladies of the United States, in settings that copy various rooms in the White House. One exhibit shows the Blue Room as it looked when Ulysses S. Grant was President. Its gold furniture was actually in use in the White House when Lincoln was President, and it was used until Franklin Roosevelt was elected in 1932.

All the figures in the rooms are dressed in clothes that belonged to the First Ladies themselves. Abigail Adams' dress is blue, with a white lace collar. Mrs. Dwight D. Eisenhower's inaugural gown is pink taffeta. The figure representing the wife of President William McKinley is wearing satin covered with pearls.

Of course the Smithsonian Institution is not just one museum. It is what is called a complex of museums—twelve of them—seven situated on the Mall, four in other parts of Washington, and one in New York City.

In the complex are Washington's Museum of Natural History, its Museum of History and Technology, and its Air and Space Museum with its popular Albert Einstein Spacearium.

The Museum of African Art, behind the Supreme Court Building, is still another part of the complex. This museum occupies several historic houses, joined into a single building. One of the houses was the home of Frederick Douglass, the son of a slave who was one of the leaders in the fight to end slavery. Groups of schoolchildren who come here are allowed to put on some of the museum's African costumes, and beat on African drums while they learn to chant and dance to African rhythms.

Among the other buildings under the big "umbrella" of the Smithsonian Institution are the National Gallery of Art and the Hirshhorn Museum.

This amazing Institution has also sent out, or sponsored, some 2,000 scientific expeditions. It operates an astrophysical laboratory in Cambridge, Massachusetts, in cooperation with Harvard University. There is a Smithsonian Tropical Research Institution in Panama, and a Radiation Biology Laboratory in Maryland. The Institution also publishes a magazine, and operates the National Zoological Park, Washington's own zoo and one of the finest in the world.

These giant pandas are favorites
at the National Zoological Park.

IN MEMORY OF FOUR PRESIDENTS

The 555-foot (169 m) marble-faced monument to George Washington, the tallest structure in the city and the tallest stone structure in the world, is the first thing most visitors see when they approach the capital.

Visitors—especially young ones—used to enjoy testing their stamina by walking up and down the 898 steps inside the hollow column. But when the number of daily visitors rose into the thousands, during the busiest spring and summer tourist seasons, the walkers caused such a traffic jam on the stairs that new regulations were made. Today everyone who wishes to reach the top of the monument—the view from there is one of the city's most popular attractions—must take the elevator's 70-second trip.

But those who wish to walk down the stairs may still do so, pausing on the way to read the inscriptions carved on nearly 200 of the stones set into the interior walls. Those stones are gifts from people who wanted to help build a memorial to George Washington. Some came from groups of students, others from states of the Union and the ruling powers of foreign lands. The Cherokee Indians sent a stone. So did the stonecutters of Philadelphia. And 30,000 people contributed one dollar each to help pay for the monument.

The first stones were put in place in 1848. But not long afterward, several things happened to delay the completion of

A view of the Washington Monument
from the Jefferson Memorial

the work. The shaft was about one-third finished when the Civil War began, for example, and no work was done on it during the years of the conflict. Then, when peace came, there was no money in the building fund. Work did not start again until Congress voted a large sum to pay for materials and masons' wages. In 1865 the army's engineers, who took over the supervision of the job, discovered that the partly-finished monument had tilted slightly. So they had to build a new foundation under the old one, and straighten the column before they could proceed.

The marble used to complete the shaft did not quite match the stone that had been used for the lower portion. That difference in color, which still shows today, tells visitors how much of the monument was built before the Civil War, and how much of it was built afterward.

A big public celebration was held when the monument was finally opened to the public in 1888. And today, once a year, a great display of fireworks is set off at the base of the shaft to mark Washington's birthday on February 22.

The monument to Thomas Jefferson, Washington's friend and the third President of the United States, was not completed until 1943, two centuries after Jefferson's birth. This open white-domed rotunda, facing the pond-like body of water called the Tidal Basin, was planned along the lines of Jefferson's own design for a rotunda at the University of Virginia.

Daniel Chester French's statue of Lincoln looks down at visitors to the Lincoln Memorial.

The words carved on its interior panels were written by Jefferson, and include the opening of the second paragraph of the Declaration of Independence: "We hold these truths to be self-evident: that all men are created equal . . ."

A 19-foot (5.8-m) bronze statue of Jefferson stands inside the rotunda, facing north, so that Jefferson is looking past the Washington Monument and straight at the distant White House.

The white marble Lincoln Memorial, which looks rather like a temple of ancient Greece, was not finished until 1922, although talk of building a memorial to Lincoln began soon after his death. The statue of his seated figure, by the American sculptor Daniel Chester French, is one of the most famous in the world. The building's thirty-six imposing columns represent the number of states in the Union at the time Lincoln died. Among the words carved on its walls are those of his Gettysburg Address, which began, "Four score and seven years ago . . ."

More than 80 billion of the coins called Lincoln pennies carry an engraving of Lincoln's head on one side, and an engraving of his beautiful memorial on the other.

The memorial to John F. Kennedy is very different from those erected to Washington, Jefferson, and Lincoln. People who visit it can hear a concert or an opera, watch a play or ballet or movie, or attend a public meeting. This memorial is just what its name suggests. It is the John F. Kennedy Center for the Performing Arts.

A Washington center for the performing arts had been dreamed of for many years before 1958, when President Eisenhower signed a bill to authorize such a building—and when Kennedy was a forty-one-year-old senator from Massachusetts. But finding funds for the center was still a problem when Kennedy, a great admirer of the arts, was elected President two years later. He established a committee to raise funds for it, and soon $13 million had been contributed by individuals, groups, and organizations.

After President Kennedy's assassination, in 1963, the Congress and people of the grieving nation raised the rest of the money needed to build a $30 million center that by then was planned to be Kennedy's memorial.

The gleaming white building, begun in 1966 and finished in 1971, stands along the Potomac River on the edge of the fashionable Georgetown section of Washington. Its main lobby, called the Grand Foyer, is 630 feet (192 m) long. The eighteen crystal chandeliers hanging from its lofty ceiling, each weighing a ton, were a gift from Sweden. Belgium presented the hall's huge mirrors.

Many of the striking features in the three theaters that open off this lobby, and in other halls of the enormous building, were presented by foreign governments. The red and gold curtains in the opera house were a gift from Japan. Canada gave the red and black woven wood curtain used in the theater. Austria, Norway, and Ireland sent chandeliers. France and the African nations of Lesotho and Senegal gave tapestries. All those gifts and many others, like the building itself, are expressions of regard for the assassinated President.

FOREIGN FLAGS ON THE
MAP OF WASHINGTON

On some maps of Washington's Northwest section, tiny flags mark the location of about 130 foreign embassies. A part of Sixteenth Street used to be called Embassy Row because so

An aerial photo of Kennedy Center (left)
with Theodore Roosevelt Bridge in the foreground

many foreign diplomatic offices stood along it. Today that name is usually applied instead to Massachusetts Avenue, where so many of the newer embassy buildings now stand. Visitors can recognize the embassies because each one flies its own national flag. The beautiful mosque, built by the Moslem nations that send representatives to Washington, is also on Massachusetts Avenue.

Sometimes a foreign ambassador lives in a mansion that also houses his embassy's office. But sometimes an embassy staff is so large that it needs a special building to work in. Many such buildings, called chancelleries, have been built in recent years. Some of them are as large as a big office building. The People's Republic of China needed so much space that it purchased a hotel to serve as its embassy.

Some members of the foreign diplomatic group send their children to special schools which teach them in their own language—French, perhaps, or Spanish, or Russian. This is one way the members of the group keep their own habits and customs alive while they live in the United States.

Each foreign group also celebrates its own national holidays. One of the most important events in Washington's busy social season, for example, is the party given by the French embassy on July 14, a French national holiday.

OUT-OF-DOORS IN WASHINGTON

In April, Washington's Japanese cherry trees burst into pink and white bloom around the edge of the Tidal Basin—the quiet pool between the Mall and the Potomac River. The first eighty trees planted around this pool were a gift to the national capital from President William Howard Taft's wife, who had admired the cherry trees she once saw blooming in Japan. Then three thousand more trees were presented to Washington by the city of Tokyo. Now, each year, thousands of visitors come to see Washington's cherry trees blossom. A Cherry Blossom Queen is crowned at a festival held on the steps of the Jefferson Memorial. There is a parade too, and all sorts of festivities.

The many gardens of Washington are at their best in the spring. One favorite of visitors is the courtyard of the Hall of the Americas, in the Pan American Union, headquarters of the Organization of American States, an alliance of all the countries of North, Central, and South America. The white marble building is given a Latin American appearance by its balconies of black ironwork and its roof of red tile. In its inner courtyard there are banana, coffee, rubber, and papaya trees growing around a fountain. In back of the building is the Aztec Garden, watched over by a statue of the Aztec god Xochipilli.

Other favorites are the Kenilworth Aquatic Gardens with their pools of lotuses and water lilies, and the Bishop's Garden beside the unfinished Cathedral Church of St. Peter and St. Paul. This building, where masons and stonecutters have been at work since 1907, welcomes people of all faiths to worship in its chapels and wander through its grounds high on a wooded hill overlooking the city.

The historic Chesapeake and Ohio Canal in Georgetown is a popular recreation area. Mule-drawn barges travel the canal in summer, and picnickers, bicyclists, and hikers use the canal's towpath.

The people of Washington spend a great deal of time out-of-doors. They often attend outdoor concerts on summer evenings, some given by the bands of the armed services at the Jefferson Memorial.

The U.S. Marine Drum and Bugle Corps, in scarlet and white, plays for the Sunset Parade each Friday all summer, in front of the old barracks where it is quartered. Opposite the barracks stands the home of the Marine Corps Commander, the oldest official Washington residence that has been lived in continuously since it was built. Once, it is said, the Marine Commander left a sign on the door when he was called away. The sign read, "Have gone to Florida to fight the Indians. Back when war is over."

Wherever people live or work in Washington, there is a park nearby. Even in the heart of the city, government workers can play ball and eat their lunch at noon on the Ellipse, the oval of green grass in front of the White House.

The National Park Service of the Department of the Interior takes care of the city's parks, and plans an outdoor program for city residents each year. National Park Service historians lead people on tours of historic sights. They may take them on walks through the old streets of Georgetown, or to the famous Custis-Lee Mansion across the Potomac in Virginia.

This house, high on a hill, was built by Martha Washington's grandson, whose daughter married Robert E. Lee. When Lee resigned from the army to join the Confederacy at the beginning of the Civil War, the house was seized and held by Union forces. After the war, the grounds around it became Arlington Cemetery, where the nation's war dead are buried. Here, before the Tomb of the Unknown Soldier, a single soldier walks sentry duty. With elaborate salutes and a clicking of heels, there is a changing of the guard every half hour during daylight, less often at night.

Most of the parks in Washington are neatly cared for. But in the largest of all, Rock Creek Park, there is a place where a stream tumbles over jagged rocks, and ancient trees rise out of a tangle of vines. The modern city of Washington becomes more crowded each year. But that one patch of wild woodland still remains, to remind Americans of the time when Abigail Adams came to Washington and found herself in the middle of a wilderness.

VISIT TO MOUNT VERNON

Fifteen miles (24 km) south of Washington, along the Potomac, stands Mount Vernon, the peaceful white plantation house where George Washington lived as a young man and where he ended his days.

Not all of his possessions are here. The field kit he used during the Revolution is in the Smithsonian Institution. Many things that belonged to him are preserved in the George Washington Masonic National Memorial Temple in Alexandria, Virginia, built by American Masons in honor of the most famous member of their society. Still other Washington mementos are in other museums in other parts of the country.

But today this gracious house is furnished much as it was when Washington lived here. The neat gardens, with their brick walks, look as they did then. So do the stables and the carriage house and the whitewashed servants' quarters. Spinning wheels still stand in the spinning room, where ten women

once spun the wool and flax for the Washington family's clothes and linens. In Washington's own bedroom is the canopied bed in which he died.

Most people who visit Washington also visit Mount Vernon. Here they can see how people lived when the nation's capital was founded. Here they can see the kind of planned order that Washington himself liked, and which he must have hoped the French engineer, L'Enfant, would put into his design for a new federal city. Here, on the brick-paved porch overlooking the Potomac, Washington probably studied L'Enfant's plan, or the copy of it made by Benjamin Banneker.

At that time the nation was a struggling handful of weak states. Today it is greater than even Washington dreamed it might become. And today the green and white city that L'Enfant planned, the capital named in honor of the father of his country, is truly "a city magnificent enough to grace a great nation."

Mount Vernon

INDEX